"If you enjoy this book
and write your review o
Thank yo

"Greetings, O Son of Wodin!"

"Greetings, O Daughter of Wodin!"

# Norse Tales

## Bit 1

Adapted by Tru Keesey

1st Edition

"Greetings, O Son of Thor!"

"Greetings, O Daughter of Thor!"

Copyright 2014 by Truman Keesey

The *Oera Linda Book* is the oldest writing of our folk.

# 4,000 Years Ago

Once there was a folk who were all tall and blond. Among them, each burg had a teacher who was a virgin (maiden). The teachers were called "burgmaids". A dead woman named "Frya" was thought of as their ghostly mother.

The top maiden, over all the folkdoms was called "The Folksmother" or "The Mother".

## THIS IS WRITTEN ON THE WARABURG BY THE ALDERGAMUDE

*"Aldergamude" is the mouth of the Alderga River.*

## Thus Is the Foretale.

Hills, bow your heads; weep, you streams and clouds. Yes. Schoonland blushes, a beslaven folk tramples on your clothing, O Frya.

*Schoonland is Scandinavia.*

*"Beslaven" – made to be slaves.*

## This Is the Tale.

One hundred and one years after the sinking of Aldland a folk came out of the East. That folk was driven by another.

*"Aldland" means "old land" which is a name for Doggerland. It sank in 2193 B.C..*

Behind us, in Twiskland, they fell into bickering, sundered themselves into two sets, and each went its own way.

*Twiskland is now Germany, at the time, of this keying.*

*"Sunder" – separate.*

Of the one no tale has come to us, but the other came in the back of our Schoonland, which was thinly settled, more thinly in the upper bit, in the heights.

Therefore they were able to take hold of it without fighting, and as they did no other harm, we would not make war about it. Now that we have learned to know them, we will tell of their ways, and after that how things went between us.

They were not wild folk, like most of Finda's folk; but, like the Egyptians, they have priests and also carven manikins in their halls of worshipping.

> *Finda was the mother of all, of those, who today's younger folk call "Asiatics", such as Vietnamese, Chinese, Korean, or Japanese, in the time of this keying.*
>
> *"Manikin" – statue.*

The priests are the only drovers over the folk; they call themselves Magyar, and their headman Magy.

> *A drove is a set of beasts who are driven. A drover is the one who drives them.*

He is high priest and king in one. The rest of the folk are of no worth, and are underyoken beneath them.

*A yoke is a stiff neck collar to harness beasts to do work.*

This folk have not even a name; but we call them Finns, for that, although all the gatherings are sad and bloody, those gatherings are so pretty that we are beneath them in that way.

*"For that" is our way of saying "because".*

But still they are not to be looked at with longing to be like them, for that they are slaves to their priests, and still more to their beliefs.

They believe that evil ghosts abound everywhere, and go into men and beasts, but of Wr-alda's ghost they know nothing.

*"Wr-alda" means "Most old", "the Oldest One", whom we know as "Breathgiver".*

They have weapons of stone, the Magyar of copper. The Magyar boast that they can cast out and call back the evil ghosts, and this frightens the folk, so that you never see a cheerful face.

When they were well set up, the Magyar sought our friendship.

They praised our speech and ways, our cattle and iron weapons, which they would willingly have traded for their gold and silver spangles, and they always kept their folk within their own boundaries, and that outwitted our watchfulness.

*Spangles are ornaments.*

Eighty years afterwards, just at the time of the Juulfeest, they overran our land like a snowstorm driven by the wind.

All who could not flee away were killed. Frya was appealed to, but the Schoonlanders had not heeded her rede. Then all the warmight was gathered, and three hours from Godasburg they were withstood, but war went on.

*"Rede" is our word for advice.*

*"Heed" means to listen and to follow advice.*

Kat or Katerine was the name of the Burgmaid, of Godasburg. Kat was proud and haughty, and would neither seek rede nor help from the mother; but when the the folk of the burg knew this, they themselves sent tellers to Texland to tell to the Folksmother.

*"Haughty" means "high" or "uppity", such as "I'm better than you are".*

Minna—this was the name of the mother—summoned all the sailors and the young men from Eastflyland and Denmark.

From this trip the tale of Wodin sprang, which is written on the strongholds, and is here given:

At Alderga Mouth, at the mouth of the Alderga River, there lived an old sea-king whose name was Sterik, and whose deeds were well known.

This old fellow had three nephews. Wodin, the eldest, lived at Lumkamakia, near the Eemude, in Eastflyland, with his father and his mother. He had once led a warhost. Teunis and Inka were warriors at sea, and were just then staying with their father at Alderga Mouth.

*A host is a big crowd.*

When the young warriors had gathered together, they picked Wodin to be their leader or king, and the men of the fleet chose Teunis for their sea-king and Inka for the headman of their fleet.

The fleet then sailed to Denmark, where they took on board Wodin and his hearty host.

The wind was fair, so they made land straightway in Schoonland. When the northern brothers met together, Wodin divided his mighty warhost into three bodies. Frya was their war-cry, and they drove back the Finns and Magyar like children.

When the Magy heard how his hosts had been utterly won against, he sent tellers with staff and kingly headgear, who said to Wodin: "O almighty king we are guilty, but all that we have done was done from need.

"You think that we made onslaught against your brothers out of ill will, but we were driven out by our foes, who are still at our heels.  We have often asked your Burgmaid for help, but she took no heed of us.

"The Magy says that if we kill half our sum of folks in fighting against each other, then the wild shepherds will come and kill all the rest.

"The Magy owns great wealth but he has seen that Frya is much more mighty than all our ghosts together.

"He will lay down his head in her lap.  You are the most warlike king on the earth, and your folk are of iron.  Become our king, and we will all be your slaves.  What mighty brightness it would be for your fame if you could drive back the wild men!

"Our horns would give forth noise with fair telling about you, and the shouting of your deeds would go before you everywhere."

*"Fair" = "pleasant, bright, complimentary".*

Wodin was strong, threatening, and warlike, but he was not clear-sighted, therefore he was taken in their toils, and bekinged by the Magy.

*"Be-" takes any noun and makes it into a verb.*

Very many of the sailors and warriors to whom this doing was disliked went away hiddenly, taking Kat with them. But Kat, who did not wish to show herself before either the mother or the folkmoot, jumped overboard.

> *Folkmoot is same as a parliament or thing. Also called "moot".*

Then a storm arose and drove the ships upon the banks of Denmark, with the total wrecking of their crews. This strait was afterwards called the Kattegat.

When Wodin was bekinged, he made onslaught against the wild men, who were all horsemen, and fell upon Wodin's host like a hailstorm; but like a whirlwind they were turned back, and did not dare to show themselves again.

When Wodin went back, Magy gave, to him, his daughter to wife.

Whereupon he was bewildered with herbs; but they were treacherous herbs, and by steps he became so bold that he dared to turn away from and slander the ghosts of Frya and Wr-alda, while he bent his free head before the untrue manikins.

*"Bewilder" – "be" =" thoroughly" + "led astray into the wilderness".*

His kingship lasted seven years, and then he was no longer seen. The Magy said that he was taken up by their gods and still bore sway over us, but our folk laughed at what they said.

*"Sway" = "control, overlordship".*

When Wodin had been unseen some time, strife arose. We wished to pick another king, but the Magy would not allow it. He said that it was his right given, to him, by his manikins.

But besides this strife there was one between the Magyar and Finns, who would worship neither Frya nor Wodin; but the Magy did just as he would, for that his daughter had a son by Wodin, and he would have it that this son was of high birth.

While all were striving and talking against each other, he bekinged the boy, and set up himself as guardian and redegiver. Those who cared more for themselves than for righteousness let him to work his own way, but the good men took their leaving.

Many Magyar fled back with their warhost, and the sea-folk took ship, with a body of stalwart Finns as rowers.

# 3,600 Years Ago

### From Minno's Writings.

When Nyhelennia, whose real name was Min-erva, was well set up, and the Krekalanders loved her as well as our own folk did, there came some highborns and priests to her stronghold and asked Min-erva where her holdings lay.

*"Ny" means "new" and "hel" means "bright".*

*"Krekaland" means "Greek Land".*

*"Highborn" = someone born into a family that has sway over others, or into a family that has higher moral qualities, depending upon the context.*

Hellenia answered, "I bear my holdings in my own bosom. What I have gotten through my forefathers is the love of wisdom, righteousness, and freedom. If I lose these I shall become as the least of your slaves; now I give rede for nothing, but then I should sell it".

The gentlemen went away laughing and saying, "Your humble servants, wise Hellenia". But they missed their aim, for the folk took up this name as a name of bright fame.

When they saw that their shot had missed they began to belittle her, and to say that she had bewitched the folk; but our folk and the good Krekalanders understood at once that it was untrue belittling.

She was once asked, "If you are not a witch, what is the use of the eggs that you always bear with you?".

Min-erva answered, "These eggs are the tokens of Frya's rede, in which our hereafter and that of the whole mankind lies hidden. Time will hatch them, and we must watch that no harm happen to them".

*"Tokens" = "symbols".*

The priests said, "Well answered; but what is the use of the dog on your right hand?"

Hellenia answered, "Does not the shepherd have a sheep-dog to keep his flock together? What the dog is to the shepherd I am in Frya's work. I must watch over Frya's flocks."

"We understand that very well," said the priests; "but tell, to us, what means the owl that always sits upon your head, is that light-shunning bird a token of your unblocked sight?"

"No," answered Hellenia; "he beminds me that there are folks on earth who, like him, have their homes in worshipping halls and holes,

"who go about in the twilight, not, like him, to warden us from mice and other scathes, but to think up swindles to steal away the knowledge of other folks, in order to overbear them, to make slaves of them, and to suck their blood like leeches."

*"Scathe" or "Skathe" or "Skathi" means "harm" or "injury".*

Another time they came with a whole host of folks, when the sickness of death was in the land, and said; "We are all making gifts to the gods that they may take away the sickness.

"Will you not help to turn away their wrath, or have you yourself brought the sickness into the land with all your arts?"

"No, said Min-erva; I know no gods that do evil, therefore I cannot ask them to do better.

"I know only one good spirit, that is Wr-alda's; and as he is good be never does evil."

"Where, then, does evil come from?" asked the priests.

"All the evil comes from you, and from the dullness of the folk who let themselves be swindled by you."

"If, then, your god is so much more good, why does he not drive away the bad?" asked the priests.

Hellenia answered: "Frya has put us here, and the bearer, that is, Time, must do the rest.

"For all bad hap there is rede and fixing to be found, but Wr-alda wills that we should seek it out ourselves, so that we may become strong and wise.

"If we will not do that, he leaves us to our own means, so that we may feel the ends of wise or foolish deeds."

Then a highborn said, "I should think it best to yield".

"Very haply", answered Hellenia; "for then men would be like sheep, and you and the priests would take care of them, shearing them and leading them to the shambles.

*Shambles is a spot where beasts are butchered.*

"This is what our god does not want, he wants that we should help one another, but that all should be free and wise."

"That is also our wont, and therefore our folk pick their reeves, border headmen, redegivers, headmen, and kings among the wisest of the good men, in order that every man shall do his best to be wise and good.

*A reeve is a foreman who works for a king.*

"Thus doing, we learn ourselves and teach the folk that being wise and doing wisely can alone lead to holiness."

"That seems very good reckoning," said the priests; "but if you mean that the sickness is made by the dullness of our minds, then Nyhellenia will perhaps be so good as to bestow upon us a little of that new light of which she is so proud".

"Yes," said Hellenia, "but ravens and other birds of prey feed only on dead flesh, whereas the sickness feeds not only on dead flesh, but on bad laws and ways and wicked lusts.

*A lust is any kind of desire or longing.*

"If you wish the sickness to quit you and not to come back, you must put away your bad lusts and become clean within and without."

"We own that the rede is good", said the priests, "but how shall we coax all the folk under our sway to keep to it?"

*"Own" here means "admit, confess".*

Then Hellenia stood up and said:

"The sparrows follow the sower, and the folk their good highborns, therefore it becomes you to begin by making yourselves to be clean, so that you may look within and without, and not be ashamed of your own ways.

*Sowing means to put seeds into soil.*

"Now, instead of cleaning the folk, you have thought up foul gatherings, in which they have so long yielded themselves that they wallow like swine in the mire to atone for your evil lusts."

The folk began to mock and to jeer, so that she did not dare to follow the thought; and one would have thought that they would have called all the folk together to drive us out of the land;

but no, in place of talking ill of her they went all about from the heathenish Krekaland to the Alps,

telling forth that it had gladdened the Almighty God to send his clever daughter Min-erva, named Nyhellenia, over the sea in a cloud to give, to folks, good rede, and that all who listened to her should become wealthy and happy, and in the end kings of all the kingdoms of the earth.

*Heathen is one or a set of folks who worships where the heather is to be found, that is out in the woods and fields. This meaning has been expanded to mean all who worship manikins.*

*"Alp" means any mountain.*

They built carven manikins to her on all their holy tables, they told forth and sold to the trusting folks rede that she had never given, and told of wonders that she had never done.

They cunningly made themselves to be knowers of our laws and ways, and by craft and swindles were able to teach and spread them around.

They set up priestesses under their own care, who were seemingly under the warding of Fasta, our first Folksmother, to watch over the foddik;

but that lamp they lit themselves, and instead of inputting the priestesses with wisdom, and then sending them to watch the sick and teach the young, they made them to be dull and unknowing, and never allowed them to come out.

*Foddik was a kind of lamp that was swung like a hand-held incense burner, hanging from chains. The ongoing flame, by their traditions, must be lit only from the ongoing flame of Frya in Texland.*

*Fasta is the original of Vesta.*

They were put to work as redegivers, but the rede which seemed to come from them was but the telling over of the behests of the priests.

*"Behest" is our way of saying "command".*

When Hellenia or Min-erva died, the priests made sham as if to be with us, and to make it to seem so, they treated Hellenia's tale as though she were a goddesse.

They would not have any other mother to be picked, saying that they feared there was no one among her maidens whom they could trust as they had trusted Minerva, called Nyhellenia.

But we would not think of Min-erva as a goddesse, for that she herself had told us that no one could be all good except the spirit of Wr-alda. Therefore we chose Geert Pyre's daughter for our mother.

When the priests saw that they could not fry their herrings on our fire, they left Athens, and said that we refused to acknowledge Min-erva as a goddess out of spite, for that she had shown so much caring to the folk of the land.

Thereupon they gave, to the folk, carven manikins of her, saying that they might ask of them whatever they liked, as long as they were driven by her. By these kinds of tales the dull witted folk were made to dislike us, and at last they made onslaught against us….

# 2,300 Years Ago

## The Writings

## Of Frethorik and Wiljow

MY name is Frethorik, my father's kind is called oera Linda, which means over the Linden. In Ljndwardia I was picked as Asga.

*"J" here was used as a vowel, and is spoken as "i" or "y".*

Ljndwardia is a new hamlet within the stronghold of the Ljudgaarda, of which the name has fallen into ill fame.

In my time much has happened. I had written a good deal about it, but afterwards much more was told to me. I will write a tale of both one and the other after this book, to add brightness to the fame of the good folks and to darken the name of the bad.

In my youth I heard gripes on all sides. The bad time was coming; the bad time did come—Frya had forsaken us. She withheld from us all her watch-maidens, for that uncanny carven manikins had been found within our landmarks.

> *"Canny" means "natural, wholesome". "Uncanny" can mean "spooky" or "disgusting", because things that are spooky or disgusting are unnatural, or it is unnatural to be exposed to them. Sometimes "canny" means "smart, intelligent, clever".*

I burnt with lust to see those manikins. In our neighbourhood a little old woman tottered in and out of the houses, always calling out about the bad times.

I came to her; she stroked my chin; then I became bold, and asked her if she would show, to me, the bad times and the manikins. She laughed good-heartedly, and took me to the stronghold. An old man asked me if I could read and write.

"No", I said. "Then you must first go and learn, he answered, otherwise it may not be shown to you. I went daily to the writer and learnt.

Eight years afterwards I heard that our Burgmaid had been unchaste, and that some of the folks of the burg had done untroth with the Magy, and many folks did it. Everywhere bickering arose.

*"Troth" means "honesty", "honor", "lawfulness", "goodness".*

There were children going against their parents; good folks were hiddenly slain. The little old woman who had brought everything to light was found dead in a ditch. My father, who was a judge, would have her to be settled for. He was killed in the night in his own house.

Three years after that the Magy was in sway without any fighting. The Saxmen had stayed lawful and upright. All the good folks fled to them. My mother died of it.

Now I did like the others. The Magy prided himself upon his cunning, but Irtha made him to know that she would not brook any Magy nor uncanny manikin on the holy bosom that had borne Frya.

*Irtha is Earth.*

As a wild horse tosses his mane after he has thrown his rider, so Irtha shook her greenwoods and her alps.

Rivers flowed over the land; the sea raged; alps spouted fire to the clouds, and what they barfed and chundered forth the clouds flung upon the earth.

At the beginning of the month of harvesting, the earth bowed towards the north, and sank down lower and lower.

In the month of winter, the low lands of Fryasland were buried under the sea. The woods in which the manikins were, were torn up and scattered by the wind.

The following year the frost came in January, and laid Fryasland hidden under a sheet of ice. In February there were storms of wind from the north, driving alps of ice and stones.

When the spring-tides came the earth raised herself up, the ice melted; with the ebb the forests with the manikins drifted out to sea. In the May, every one who dared went to home. I came with a maiden to the stronghold Liudgaarde. How sad it looked there.

The greenwoods of the Lindaoorden were almost all gone. Where Liudgaarde used to be was sea. The waves swept over the walls of the stronghold. Ice had wrecked the high building, and the houses lay heaped over each other.

On the slope of the dyke I found a stone on which the writer had written his name. That was a sign to me. The same thing had happened to other strongholds as to ours. In the upper lands they had been wrecked by the earth, in the lower lands by the water.

Fryasburg, at Texland, was the only one found unscathed, but all the land to the north was sunken under the sea, and has never been gotten back.

At the mouth of the Flymeer, as we were told, thirty salty swamps were found, made of the greenwoods and the ground that had been swept away. At Westflyland there were fifty.

The waterway which had run through the land from Alderga was filled up with sand and wrecked. The seafaring folks and other wayfarers who were at home had kept themselves, their goods, and their kindred upon their ships.

> *"Fare" means to travel. "Way" means "road" or "path".*

But the black people at Lydasburg and Alkmarum had done the same; and as they went south they kept many girls, and as no one came to own them, they took them for their wives.

The folks who came back all lived within the boundaries of the stronghold, as outside there was nothing but mud and marsh.

The old houses were all smashed together. Folks bought cattle and sheep from the upper lands, and in the great houses where erst the maidens were set up, cloth and felt were made for a livelihood. This happened 1888 years after the sinking of Atland.

> *"Erst" means "at first" or "earlier".*

For 282 years we had not had a Folksmother, and now, when everything seemed to be lost, they set about picking one. The lot fell upon Gosa, whos kind was named Makonta from her forefathers. She was Burgmaid at Fryasburg, in Texland.

She had a clear head and strong understanding, and was very good; and as her stronghold was the only one that had been spared, every one saw in that her calling. Ten years after that the seafarers came from Forana and Lydasburg.

They wished to drive the black men, with their wives and children, out of the land. They wished to get the rede of the mother about their wishing. She asked them:

"Can you send them all back to their land? If so, then lose no time, or they will find no kindred alive".
'No", they said.

Gosa answered: "They have eaten your bread and salt; they have put themselves wholly under your warding.

*"Bread and salt" is an old ritual of friendship.*

"You must take rede from your own hearts. But I will give, to you, one bit of rede. Keep them till you are able to send them back, but keep them outside your strongholds.

"Watch over their righteousness, and teach them as if they were Frya's sons. Their women are the strongest here. Their blood will disappear like smoke, till at last nothing but Frya's blood will stay in their children."

So they stayed here. Now, I should wish that my children should see in how far Gosa spoke the truth.

When our land began to be be healed, there came hosts of poor Saxon men and women to the neighbourhoods of Staveren and Alderga, to seek after gold and other wealth in the swampy lands.

But the sea-folks would not allow it, so they went and settled in the empty hamlet of the West Flyland to keep their lives.

## 2,200 Years Ago

Writer is unknown, but probably son or grandson of Beden.

I will first write about black Adel. Black Adel was the fourth king after Friso. In his youth he studied first at Texland, and then at Staveren, and afterwards fared through all the folkdoms.

> *Among the folks of northern Europe, to call someone "black" meant that they were white folks with black hair, such as "The Black Douglas", or "Halfdan the*

*Black", or "Olaf the Black". There were also black folks in our tale but they are called "black folks" and not associated with a particular name.*

When he was twenty-four years old his father had him elected Asega-Asker. As soon as be became Asker he always took the side of the straitened and needy. The wealthy, he said, do enough of wrong by means of their wealth, therefore we ought to take care that the needy look up to us.

*A strait is a tight spot, a squeezed or pinched position, used to tell of lack of supply or money. In navigation a strait is a narrow passage of water between two bits of land, such as the Strait of Magellan.*

By speaking of this kind he became the friend of the stricken and the fear of the wealthy. It was taken so far that his father looked up to him. When his father died he took his spot, and then he wished to keep his own job as well, as the kings of the East used to do.

*"Looked up to him" he became more important than his father.*

The wealthy would not bear this, so all the folk rose up, and the wealthy were glad to get out of the gathering with whole skins. From that time there was no more talk of fairness. He overbore the wealthy and flattered the needy, by whose help he won in all his wishes.

King Askar, as he was always called, was seven feet high, and his strength was as unusual as his height. He had bright thinking, so that he understood all that was talked about, but in his deeds he did not show much wisdom.

He had a handsome face and a smooth tongue, but his soul was blacker than his hair. When he had been king for a year, he made all the young men in the state to come once a year to the field to have a sham fight.

At first he had some stickiness with it, but at last it became such a wonted way that old and young came from all sides to ask if they might have a hand in it. When he had brought it this far, he set up schools of warcraft.

The wealthy griped that their children no longer learned to read and write. Askar paid no heed to it; but shortly afterwards, when a sham fight was held, he went onto a throne and spoke aloud:

"The wealthy have come to bellyache to me that their boys do not learn to read and write. I answered nothing; but I will now tell forth my thoughts, and let the overall gathering pick."

While they all looked at him with a wanting to know, he said further:

"By my thinking, we ought to leave reading and writing now to the maidens and wise folks.

"I do not wish to speak ill of our forefathers; I will only say that in the times so boasted of by some, the Burgmaids brought in bickerings into our land, which the mothers were unable, either first or last, to put an end to.

"Worse still, while they talked and chattered about useless ways the Gauls came and took all our comely southern land.

> *Gauls are the same as Gaels or Ghouls, the Druid priests come up from Chaldea, with their followers.*

"Even at this very time our fallen brothers and their warriors have already come over the Scheldt. It therefore is for us to pick whether we will bear a yoke or a sword.

"If we wish to be and to stay free, it behoves our young men to leave reading and writing alone for a time; and instead of playing games of swinging and wrestling, they must learn to play with sword and spear.

> *Behove, behoove – same. "Become" could also be used as in "make to be comely". "Comely" = "handsome", "beautiful", "agreeable", "satisfactory".*

"When we will be wholly ready, and the boys will be big enough to carry helmet and shield and to use their weapons, then, with your help, I will make onslaught against the foe.

"The Gauls may then write of the winning against their helpers and warriors upon our fields with the blood that flows from their wounds.

"When we will have once driven out the foe, then we must follow it up till there will be no more Gauls, Slaves, nor Tartars to be driven out of Frya's odals. That is right, the majority shouted, and the wealthy did not dare to open their mouths."

*"Odal" = land gotten through one's forebears, or land owned by an individual or a family.*

He must surely have thought over this speech and had it written out, for on the evening of the same day there were likenesses of it in at least twenty sundry hands, and they all sounded the same. Afterwards he bade the ship folks to make twofold prows, upon which steel crossbows could be set.

Those who were backward in doing this were tolled, and if they swore that they had no means, the wealthy men of the hamlet were made to give it. Now we shall see what came from all this bustle.

In the north part of Britain there is a Scotch folk—the most of them spring from Frya's blood—some of them are of the blood of the followers of Kalta, and, for the rest, from Britons and runaways who bit by bit, in the going of time, took shelter there from the mines of tin.

Those who come from the mines of tin have wives, either altogether outlandish or of outlandish forebears. They are all under the sway of the Gauls. Their weapons are wooden bows and arrows tipped with stag's-horn or flint.

Their houses are of turf and straw, and some of them live in caves in the alps. Sheep that they have stolen are their only wealth. Some of the children of

Kaltana's followers still have iron weapons, which they have gotten from their forefathers.

To make myself to be well understood, I must let alone for a while my tale of the Scotch folk, and write something about the near Krekalanders. The Krekalands erst belonged to us only, but from time out of mind children of Lyda and Finda have set themselves up there.

*"Near Krekaland" means "Near Greekland", which means the Italian peninsula and surrounding islands.*

*Lyda was the mother of all black folks.*

Of these last there came in the end a whole host from Troy. Troy is the name of a town that the far Krekalanders had taken and wrecked.

*"Far Krekaland" means "Far Greekland", the Attic peninsula and surroundings.*

When the Trojans had nestled themselves among the near Krekalanders, with time and business they built a strong town with walls and strongholds named Rome, that is, roomy.

When this was done, the folk by craft and might made themselves to be drovers of the folk of the whole land. The folk who live on the south side of the Mediterranean Sea, come for the most from Phœnicia.

The Phœnicians are a bastard spawn of the blood of Frya, Finda, and Lyda. The Lyda folk were there as slaves, but by the unchastity of the women these black folks have lowered the other folks and dyed them brown.

These folks and the Romans are ever striving for the sway over the Mediterranean Sea.

The Romans, moreover, live at strife with the Phœnicians; and their priests, who wish to take the whole sway of the earth, cannot bear the sight of the Gauls.

First they took from the Phœnicians Marseilles—then all the lands lying to the south, the west, and the north, as well as the southern part of Britain—and they have always driven away the Phœnician priests, that is the Gauls, of whom thousands have sought shelter in North Britain.

A short time ago the chief of the Gauls was set up in the stronghold, which is called Karnac, that is the corner, whence he told forth his bidding to the Gauls. All their gold was likewise taken in there.

Keeren Herne, or Kerenac, is a stronghold of stone which did belong to Kalta. Therefore the maidens of the children of Kaltana's followers wished to have the stronghold again.

*"Keeren Herne" means "Picked Corner".*

*Kalta was, though not the mother of, the gatherer of the Kelts.*

Thus through the ill will of the maidens and the Gauls, hatred and bickering spread over the alp land with fire and sword.

Our sea folks often came there to get wool, which they told out for with tanned hides and linen. Askar had often gone with them, and had hiddenly made friendship with the maidens and some highborn, and bound himself to drive the Gauls out of Kerenac.

*"Tell" or "tell out" = "pay", or "count".*

When he came back to there again he gave to the highborn and the fighting men iron helmets and steel bows. War had come with him, and soon blood was streaming down the slopes of the alps.

When Askar thought that a fair time came, he went with forty ships and took Kerenac and the headman of the Gauls, with all his gold.

The folks with whom he fought against the warriors of the Gauls, he had lured out of the Saxenmarken by offering of much booty and plunder. Thus nothing was left to the Gauls.

After that he took two islands for frolic land for his ships, from which he used later to sally forth and plunder all the Phœnician ships and towns that he could reach.

*"Frolic land" = a safe haven.*

When he came back he brought nearly six hundred of the best youths of the Scotch alpine men with him.

He said that they had been given, to him, as gripped men, that he might be sure that the forebears would stay true to him; but this was untrue. He kept them as a bodyguard at his seat, where they had daily schooling in riding and in the use of all kinds of weapons.

> *"Gripped" = "held", in other words, prisoners or hostages.*

The Denmarkers, who proudly thought themselves to be sea-warriors above all the other sea-folks, no sooner heard of the bright deeds of Askar, than they became threatened in their self-love by him to such a length, that they would bring war over the sea and over his lands.

See here, then, how he was able to forestall a war.

Among the wreckage of the smashed stronghold of Stavia there was still set up a clever Burgmaid, with a few maidens.

Her name was Reintja, and she was far known for her wisdom. This maid offered her help to Askar, if he would afterwards rebuild the stronghold of Stavia.

When he had bound himself to do this, Reintja went with three maidens to Hals. She travelled by night, and by day she made speeches in all the markets and in all the gatherings.

*Hals is Holstein.*

Wr-alda, she said, had told her by his thunder that all the Frya's folk must become friends, and become one as brothers and sisters, otherwise Finda's folk would come and sweep them off the face of the earth.

After the thunder Frya's seven watch-maidens came to her in a dream seven nights one after another [so she said].

They had said, "Bale hovers over Frya's land with yoke and chains; therefore all the folk who have sprung from Frya's blood must do away with the names of their fathers' kind, and only call themselves Frya's children, or Frya's folk.

*"Bale" = ""harm, injury, ruin, evil, mischief, wickedness, a noxious thing".*

"They must all rise up and drive Finda's folk out of Frya's odals. If you will not do that, you will bring the slave-chains round your necks, and the headmen of the outlanders will ill-treat your children and flog them till the blood streams into your graves.

"Then shall the ghosts of your forefathers come to you, and reproach your nithing and thoughtlessness."

*"Nithing" = "coward" or "cowardly". "Cower" means " hide" or" fearfully not to strike against a threat".*

The dull witted folk who, by the deeds of the Magyars, were already so much used to folly, believed all that she said, and the mothers clasped their children to their bosoms.

When Reintja had brought the king of Holstein and the others to a bond, she sent tellers to Askar, and went herself along the Baltic Sea.

From there she went to the Lithauers, so called for that they always strike at their foe's face. The Lithauers are runaways and banished folk of our own kind, who wander about in the Twisklanden.

*"Lithauers" means "hewers of faces" and means, for us, the earlier Lithuanians.*

Their wives have been mostly stolen from the Tartars. The Tartars are a branch of Finda's kind, and are thus called by the Twisklanders for that they never will be still, but stir folks to fight.

She went on beyond the Saxsenmarken, going through the other Twisklanders so as always to do again the same thing. After two years had gone by, she came along the Rhine to home.

*"Mark" = "boundary of land", plural "marken".*

Among the Twisklanders she gave herself out for a mother, and said that they might come back as free and true folks; but then they must go over the Rhine and drive the Gauls out of Frya's south lands.

If they would do that, then her King Askar would go over the Scheldt and win back the land. Among the Twisklanders many bad customs of the Tartars and Magyars have crept in, but likewise many of our laws have stayed.

Therefore they still have Maidens, who teach the children and give rede to the old. In the beginning they were against Reintja, but at last she was followed, her bidding was done, and she was talked of highly by them where it was useful or needed.

As soon as Askar heard from Reintja's tellers how the Jutlanders were bent, he straightway, on his side, sent tellers to the King of Hals.

*"Bent" = "leaning", "inclined", "wonted" "set in mind or heart".*

The ship in which the tellers went was laden with women's spangles, and took also a golden shield on which Askar's likeness was comelily shown. These tellers were to ask the King's daughter, Frethogunsta, in wedlock for Askar.

*"Laden" – past participle of verb "load".*

*"Comely" – "good looking".*

Frethogunsta came a year after that to Staveren. Among her followers was a Magy, for the Jutlanders had been long ago fallen.

Soon after Askar had wedded Frethogunsta, a house of worshipping was built at Staveren. In the house of worshipping were put uncanny manikins, bedecked with gold-woven clothes.

> *"Deck" = "adorn", "decorate". "Be-" is an intensive prefix, might be thought of as "thoroughly".*

It is also said that Askar, by night, and at unseasonable times, kneeled to them with Frethogunsta; but one thing is sure, the stronghold of Stavia was never rebuilt. Reintja was already come back, and went angrily to Prontlik the mother, at Texland, to gripe.

> *"Unseasonable" = "inappropriate", "bad time".*
> *"Season" = "a time".*

Prontlik sent out tellers in all ways and whereabouts, who told forth that Askar is gone over to worshipping of uncanny manikins. Askar took no heed of this, but unforeseen a fleet came from Hals.

In the night the maidens were driven out of the stronghold, and in the morning there was nothing to be seen of the stronghold but a glowing heap of rubbish. Prontlik and Reintja came to me for shelter.

When I thought upon it, I thought that it might show itself to be bad for my folkdom. Therefore, we hit upon a dodge which might help us all. This is the way we went to work.

*"Dodge" = "trick"*.

In the middle of the Krijlwood, to the east of Liudwerd, lies our spot of shelter, which can be reached only by a hidden path.

A long time ago I had set up a guardship of young men who all hated Askar, and kept away all other folks. Now it was come to such a pitch among us, that many women, and even men, talked about ghosts, white women, and gnomes, just like the Denmarkers.

Askar had made use of all these follies for his own behoof, and we wished to do the same. One dark night I brought the Maidens to the stronghold, and afterwards they went with their helping-maids clad in white along the path, so that nobody dare go there any more.

When Askar thought he had his hands free, he let the Magyars fare through his folkdoms under all kinds of names, and, besides in my folkdom, they were not spurned away anywhere.

After that Askar had become so bound with the Jutlanders and the Denmarkers, they all went roving together; but it yielded no real good to them.

They brought all kinds of outlandish goods to home, and just for that the young men would learn no trades, nor work in the fields; so at last he was made to take slaves; but that was altogether against Wr-alda's wish and to Frya's counsel.

Therefore the bane was sure to follow it. This is the way in which the bane came. They had all together taken a whole fleet that came out of the Mediterranean Sea. This fleet was laden with purple cloths and other wealth that came from Phœnicia.

The weak folks of the fleet were put ashore south of the Seine, but the strong folks were kept to work as slaves. The handsomest were kept ashore, and the ugly and black were kept on board ship as rowers.

In the Fly the plunder was shared, but, without their knowing it, they shared the bane too. Of those who were put in the outlandish ships six died of colic. It was thought that the food and drink were baneful, so it was all thrown overboard, but the colic stayed all the same.

Wherever the slaves or the goods came, there it came too. The Saxonmen took it over to their marches. The Jutlanders brought it to Schoonland and along the coasts of the Baltic Sea, and with Askar's seamen it was taken to Britain.

We and the folks of Grênegâ did not allow either the folks or the goods to come over our boundaries, and therefore we stayed free from it.

How many folks were borne off by this sickness I cannot tell; but Prontlik, who heard it afterwards from the maidens, told me that Askar had helped out of his folkdoms a thousand times more free-men than he had brought dirty slaves in.

When the plague had stopped, the Twisklanders who had become free came to the Rhine, but Askar would not put himself on the same worth with the highborn of that low fallen kind.

He would not put up with them to call themselves Frya's children, as Reintja had offered them, but he forgot then that he himself had black hair. Among the Twisklanders there were two tribes who did not call themselves Twisklanders.

One came from the far south-east, and called themselves Allemannen. They had given themselves this name when they had no women among them, and were wandering as putaways in the forests.

Later on they stole women from the slave folks like the Lithauers, but they kept their name.

The other tribe, that wandered about in the neighbourhood, called themselves Franks, not for that they were free, but the name of their first king was Frank, who, by the help of the fallen maidens, had had himself made to be king over his folk through the father's blood or kind.

The folk nearest to him called themselves Thioth—his sons—that is, sons of the folk. They had stayed free, for that they never would acknowledge any king, or highborn, or overlord but those picked by overall like-mindedness in a folkmoot.

Askar had already learned from Reintja that the Twisklander highborn were almost always at war with each other. He put forth to them that they should pick a duke from his folk, for that, as he said, he was afraid that they would bicker among themselves to try for the sway.

He said also that his highborn could speak with the Gauls. This, he said, was also the thinking of the mother. Then the highborn of the Twisklanders came together, and after twenty-one days they picked Alrik as duke. Alrik was Askar's nephew.

He gave, to him, two hundred Scotch and one hundred of the greatest Saksmannen to go with him as a bodyguard. The highborn were to send twenty-one of their sons as gripped men for their troth.

> *"Saksmannen" and like-sounding words all mean "Saxons".*

Thus far all had gone alike to his wishes; but when they were to go over the Rhine, the king of the Franks would not be under Alrik's word.

Thereupon all was bewilderment. Askar, who thought that all was going on well, landed with his ships on the other side of the Scheldt; but there they were already aware of his coming, and were on their guard.

He had to flee as quickly as he had come, and was himself taken. The Gauls did not know whom they had taken, so he was afterwards traded for a highborn Gaul whom Askar's folk had taken with them. While all this was going on, the Magyars went about boldly over the lands of our neighbours.

Near Egmuda, where formerly the stronghold Forana had stood, they built a house of worshipping bigger and wealthier than that which Askar had built at Staveren.

They said afterwards that Askar had lost the onslaught against the Gauls, for that the folk did not believe that Wodin's ghost could help them, and therefore they would not beg to him. They went about stealing young children, whom they kept and brought up in the mysteries of their stinking teachings.

# 1,100 Years Ago

I, Ibn Fadlan have seen the Rus as they came on their trading trips and set up their shorttime abodes by the Volga River.

I have never seen more flawless bodies, tall as date palms, blond and ruddy.

*The French word "blond" is male, "blonde" is female.*

When they have come from their land and anchored on, or tied up at the shore of the Volga, which is a great river, they built big houses of wood on the shore, each holding ten to twenty souls more or less.

When the ships come to this mooring spot, everybody goes ashore with bread, meat, onions, milk and drink and betakes himself to a long upright bit of wood that has a face like a man's and is beskirted by little carven manikins, behind which are long stakes in the ground.

The Rus bows himself before the big carving and says, "O my Lord, I have come from a far land and have with me such and such a number of girls and such and such a number of sables", and he tells a list of all his other wares.

Then he says, "I have brought, to you, these gifts," and lays down what he has brought with him, and speaks on,

"I wish that you would send, to me, a trader with many worthy disks of metal, who will buy from me whatever I wish and will not gainsay anything I say." Then he goes away.

If he has hardship selling his wares and the time of his staying is stretched, he will go back with a gift a second or third time. If he has still further hardship, he will bring a gift to all the little manikins and ask for their helping, saying,

"These are the wives of our lord and his daughters and sons." And he talks to each manikin in turn, asking for its helping and begging humbly.

Often the selling goes more easily and after selling out he says, "My Lord has fulfilled my lusts; I must give back to him,"

and he takes a set sum of sheep or cattle and slaughters them, gives a bit of the meat as alms, brings the rest and puts it before the great manikin and the little manikins around it, and hangs the heads of the cattle or sheep on the stakes.

In the night, dogs come and eat all, but the one who has made the gift says, "Truly, my lord is fair toward me and has used the gift that I brought to him."

# 900 Years Ago

A very famous house of worshipping called Uppsala was in a burg hard by Sigtuna in Sweden. The hall was bedecked with gold. The folk there worshipped three manikins that sat on a triple throne.

Thor was thought to be the mightiest. The manikin, that was thought to be Thor himself, sat in the middle throne. The manikins, that were thought to be Wodin and Freyr, were seated on the thrones to the sides of him.

The manikin, that was thought to be Freyr, was made with a great upright limb, a word that we do not use here.

The priests had put a byrnie on Wodin's manikin and in the hands, of that of Thor, they had put a rod with a spiked head.

*A byrnie is a kind of body's armor.*

Each of the three manikins has a priest set to it. Each priest made offerings to his manikin, taken from the folk.

If foodlessness or plague came, an offering was made to Thor's manikin; if there was war, an offering was made to Wodin's manikin; if a wedlock was to be made, an offering was made to Freyr.

Every nine years every folkdom of Sweden must send men and offerings to Uppsala for a gathering, under threat of harm if they did not send them.

If a folkdom had erst picked to go the Roman way, and would not worship the manikins, then they must give wealth instead, to be allowed to keep out of the gathering.

Those folkdoms, that had not taken the Roman way, must send nine men, and nine males of every kind of beast to be killed and offered to the manikins.

The dead bodies of the nine males were hung within a grove beside the house of worshipping.

The priests told folks that the grove was mightily holy. so that each tree was held to be to be holy for the death of those killed or their rotting bodies hanging there, along with the dead bodies of dogs and horses hanging among them.

There were seventy-two sundry kinds of beasts hanging within the grove.

The songs that the priests sang while offering the dead bodies were so bad, that they were sickening to be heard.

These ways, as we know, were brought in by the Magy long, long ago, and there were those wise enough to shun them.

Foolish folks believed the priests, when they told, to them, that their wishes were given, if a man, after being thrown into a nearby spring, drowned.

Men of the House of Steinkell were the kings of the Swedes in the time when the writing about the house of worshipping at Uppsala was made.

Steinkell was the first of that kingly house. His kingship was from 1060 until 1066 A.D.. Before Steinkell's house, the House of Munso were the kings of the Swedes.

Emunth the Old was the last of the house of Munso to be king. Jarl Steinkell, before he ever was picked to be king, was wedded to the daughter of Emunth. Steinkell was not fom Uppsala, as were the kings before him.

*"Jarl" is another way of saying "earl", which is a military and governmental rank just below a king. The "j" is pronounced as "i" or "y".*

Steinkell's mother's name was Astrith, daughter of Njal the son of Fin the Squinter, from Halogaland; and his father was Rognvald the Old.

Steinkell was a Jarl in Sweden at first, and then after the death of Emunth the Old, the Swedes picked him to be their King.

Then the throne passed out of the line of the olden kings of the Swedes.

Steinkell was mighty. He wedded the daughter of King Eymunth. Eymunth died in his bed in Sweden about the time that King Harold fell in England.

*"Eymunth" and "Emunth" are fillings in for the Old Swedish name "Æmunðær".*

Steinkell fell in step with the leadership of Rome, which, just as earlier priests had called themselves spokesmen for Min-Erva, made priests who called themselves spokesmen for Jesus, though they were not.

Back in Rome the high priests were doing the same kinds of offerings as in Uppsala, or very like them, but they were now doing them hiddenly, in the dark cellars of the house of worshipping, while in the daylight they did other more seemly kinds of deeds, to be seen of men.

Steinkell let the Roman henchmen in Hamburg-Bremen lay out the kind and ways of his kingship.

Naetheless, when Rome's man in Sigtuna wanted to wreck the house of worship at Uppsala, Steinkill stopped him from doing it. Steinkill thought that there would be too much fighting about it if the hall were wrecked.

It looks as though Steinkill was right about that, as later on, after his death, his son King Inge the Elder wanted to stop the offerings at Uppsala, whereupon he was sent away by the folk and was made to leave and abide afar or wander afar.

Steinkill abode mostly in Westgothland where he was long called to mind as the king who "loved West Geats before all his other underlings". He was talked of highly as a great archer whose hit spots were long shown with worship.

*"Worship" comes from "worth", which means "value". The spots that Steinkell had hit with his arrows were valued, were worshipped. Valued.*

In a speech by Thorvid, the lawspeaker of Westgothland before an onslaught against Harald Hardrada, the lawspeaker tells of the Geats' troth to Steinkill:

*Lawspeakers were men whose job was to keep the law in their minds, and to tell it forth at any moot.*

The lawspeaker of the Gautland folk, Thorvid, sat upon a horse, and the bridle was fastened to a stake that stood in the mire. He broke out with these words:

"God knows we have many brave and handsome fellows here, and we shall let King Steinkell hear that we stood by the good jarl stoutheartedly.

"I am sure of one thing: we shall behave great heartedly against these Northmen, if they make onslaught against us; but if our young folks give way, and should not stand to it, let us not run farther than to that stream;

but if they should give way farther, which I am sure they will not do, let it not be farther than to that hill."

By a legend Steinkill was buried in the "royal hill" near Levene in Westgothland. His two sons Halsten and Inge the Elder would both become kings of the Swedes.

# Enjoy the Next Book in This Set!

Send, to me, your email and I'll tell, to you, how you will get the special price!

trukeesey@verizon.net

## NORSE TALES BIT 2

### TRU KEESEY

Printed in Great Britain
by Amazon